Beth's Bed

Written by Joanne Reay
Illustrated by Tungwai Chau

SANDUSKY LIBRARY

Ben's in bed.
Ned's in bed

"I bet Ted's under the bed," says Ben.

A felt pen . . . red men . . . Ben's vest . . . an egg . . . a nest . . .

A hen . . . a shell . . . is that Beth's bell?

"Well, well! Let's get to bed," says Ned.

And Beth. And Ted.